INVESTIGATING NATURAL DISASTERS

INVESTIGATING
EARTHQUAKES

BY ELIZABETH ELKINS

CAPSTONE PRESS
a capstone imprint

Edge Books are published by Capstone Press,
1710 Roe Crest Drive, North Mankato, Minnesota 56003
www.mycapstone.com

Library of Congress Cataloging-in-Publication Data
Cataloging-in-Publication information is on file with the Library of Congress.
ISBN 978-1-5157-4038-4 (library binding)
ISBN 978-1-5157-4110-7 (paperback)
ISBN 978-1-5157-4127-5 (eBook PDF)

Editorial Credits
Alesha Sullivan, editor; Steve Mead, designer; Morgan Walters, media researcher;
Laura Manthe, production specialist

Photo Credits
Alamy: Keith Taylor, 14; Capstone Press, 16, 17; Getty Images: Dave Bartruff, 19, Ivan Konar/
CON, 21; iStockphoto: Claudiad, cover; Newscom: A3366 esa Deutsche Presse-Agentur, 26,
Everett Collection, 20, KIMIMASA MAYAMA/EPA, 12, Oxford Science Archive Heritage Images,
6; Science Source: Inga Spence, 25, Gary Hincks, 13; Shutterstock: arindambanerjee, 23, daulon,
15, dcwcreations, middle 29, Denis Burdin, 10, 11, Designua, 7, goir, bottom 29, Israel Hervas
Bengochea, 9, Nik Merkulov, design element throughout, cover, Paul Reeves Photography, 27,
SeDmi, top 29, Somjin Klong-ugkara, 5

Source Notes
Page 5: Powerful Nepal earthquake leaves heavy death toll. http://www.cbsnews.com/news/
powerful-earthquake-strikes-nepal-killing-dozens/. 25 April 2015.

Printed and bound in China.
007883

TABLE OF CONTENTS

"WE HAVE LOST OUR HISTORY"

It was just before noon on April 25, 2015, in the city of Kathmandu, Nepal. Suddenly the ground began to shake. A huge earthquake struck. It was strong enough to be felt in neighboring countries, such as India and China. By the time the quake and its **aftershocks** stopped, thousands of people had died. Most buildings there were not made to withstand earthquakes. They collapsed. Many historic monuments in Nepal, some hundreds of years old, crumbled into dust and piles of brick.

FACT

Several million earthquakes take place each year. But many are too small to feel or happen in very remote places. Only a small percentage are strong enough to cause damage.

aftershock—a small earthquake that follows a larger one

Nepalese author Shiwani Neupane wrote,

"The sadness is sinking in. We have lost our temples, our history, the places we grew up."

Residents walk near piles of rubble and collapsed buildings after the Nepal earthquake disaster.

The 2015 Nepal earthquake was one of the worst in recent history. But earthquakes have been occurring since Earth first formed. When earthquakes occur, they often cause widespread devastation and sometimes even death. And there is very little that can be done to predict them. For people who live in places where earthquakes frequently happen, they can only try to be prepared. They know that in a moment, an earthquake can strike and destroy almost everything around them.

WHAT CAUSES EARTHQUAKES

Just what makes an earthquake happen? Earth is made up of layers—the crust, the **mantle**, and the core. **Tectonic plates** are found in the lithosphere, which is a layer of Earth's crust and the solid, upper part of the mantle. The place where one plate touches another is called a plate boundary.

WEGENER'S THEORY

Alfred Wegener suggested the theory of continental drift in 1912. He believed the edges of the plates fit together like puzzle pieces. Similar rock types and fossils were found on different continents that seemed to fit together. Oceans now separate these continents. Wegener thought this proved that all land was once connected. Wegener turned out to be right. But he didn't know what caused the continents to move. Scientists now know that **convection** within Earth's layers causes plates to move.

There are three kinds of plate boundaries. Divergent plate boundaries happen in places where the plates are spreading apart. The space between the plates fills with hot liquid rock from deep in the Earth. Transform plate boundaries happen when the edges of plates slide past each other. Convergent plate boundaries happen when the edge of one plate is forced underneath the edge of another so that they seem to overlap.

Earthquakes, volcanoes, and mountains occur along these three types of plate boundaries.

Divergent plate boundary

Transform plate boundary

Convergent plate boundary

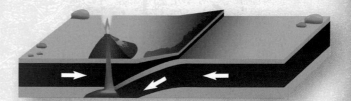

mantle—the layer of super-hot rock that surrounds Earth's core

tectonic plate—one of many gigantic slabs of Earth's crust that move around on magma

convection—the movement of heat through liquids and gases

Quakes and Plate Boundaries

Earthquakes occur when plates move at their boundaries and release energy. The strongest earthquakes appear at convergent boundaries. When the plates collide, the movement causes an earthquake. The next strongest earthquakes happen at transform boundaries, when one plate slips past another. Earthquakes at divergent boundaries aren't as strong as the other two.

Earthquakes can also happen at the cracks in the tectonic plates themselves, which are called **faults**. These faults are caused by stress in the Earth's crust from plate movement. The release of energy in one fault during an earthquake can create stress in related faults and cause a whole series of earthquakes.

FACT

The most famous fault in the United States is the San Andreas Fault in California. It connects to smaller faults. Together, they form a fault system.

fault—a crack in the earth where two plates meet; earthquakes often occur along faults

MID-ATLANTIC RISING

The Mid-Atlantic Ridge is a well-known example of a divergent plate boundary. It runs nearly the entire length of the Atlantic Ocean. The Mid-Atlantic Ridge is formed by the Eurasian Plate and the North American Plate spreading apart. Iceland lies right on top of the Mid-Atlantic Ridge. The island is slowly being pulled apart. New crust is forming on both sides of the plate boundary. Someday the Atlantic Ocean may spill in to fill up the crack. Then Iceland will become two separate islands.

The National Park of Thingvellir in Iceland is the site of a rift valley that marks the tip of the Mid-Atlantic Ridge.

Climate Change

Climate change is affecting many of Earth's systems and weather. The changes have contributed to natural disasters, such as hurricanes and floods. But climate change may have an effect on earthquakes too. Glaciers are a massive weight on the Earth's crust. When glaciers melt, this weight is reduced. Then Earth's crust can bounce back and trigger seismic activity and reactivate faults. The changes in Earth's crust put new pressure on the magma chambers of volcanoes, causing them to erupt. In places such as Greenland, where there is a huge sheet of ice melting, the change in weight could cause earthquakes. These earthquakes could also trigger underwater landslides and tidal waves.

Places like Antarctica and Greenland are home to many of Earth's glaciers.

In areas where the ocean level rises because of melting ice, flooding takes place in coastal areas. The weight of this water can put pressure on the tectonic plates. This can trigger earthquakes around the edges of major ocean **basins**. Underwater landslides can also release deposits of gas from the ocean floor, which could also lead to earthquakes.

FACT

Man-made activities such as drilling for oil or **fracking** to access natural gas can also produce earthquakes. These activities change the pressure on faults underground.

basin—the low, flat part of an ocean's floor

fracking—the process of injecting liquid at high pressure into rocks to force open existing cracks and extract oil or gas

WHAT HAPPENS AFTER

Earthquakes alone can cause a lot of damage. But they can also trigger other disasters to happen. In 2011 an earthquake took place off the coast of Tohoku, Japan. It was Japan's most powerful earthquake ever. The Tohoku earthquake was strong enough to actually move the island of Japan 8 feet (2.4 meters). It even shifted the **axis** of the Earth. But it wasn't the quake that did the most damage.

Fishing vessels washed ashore during the Japan earthquake disaster in 2011.

VOLCANOES AND EARTHQUAKES

Earthquakes can also force volcanoes to erupt. An earthquake that takes place near an active volcano can change the pressure of the hot magma in the volcano. This forces the volcano to erupt, which allows the magma to escape. The **seismic waves** created by an earthquake, even at a distance, can also change the pressure of magma. The waves can change the thickness or stir up bubbles in the magma. The "Ring of Fire" in the Pacific Ocean is a place where many earthquakes and volcanic eruptions take place together because there are many volcanoes and fault lines found there.

Ring of Fire

When the **epicenter** of an earthquake is under the ocean, it can trigger a tsunami. A tsunami is a series of huge waves that travel across the ocean and then inland, causing extensive damage. The tsunami caused by the Tohoku earthquake swept away everything in its path, from buildings and cars to people. It also damaged three nuclear reactors at the Fukushima Daiichi Nuclear Power Plant. People within 12 miles (19 kilometers) of the plant had to leave for their own safety. Almost 16,000 people died from the earthquake and tsunami combined.

axis—a straight line around which an object rotates

seismic wave—a wave of energy created by an earthquake

epicenter—the point on Earth's surface directly above the place where an earthquake occurs

EARTHQUAKE ZONES

There are places in the world where earthquakes are more likely to happen than others. This is because of the position of tectonic plates and the types of boundaries between them. Japan experiences many earthquakes because it is located in the Ring of Fire. This part of the world surrounds the basin of the Pacific Ocean. It is home to many volcanoes. Seismic activity is common there because the massive Pacific Tectonic Plate interacts with many smaller, lighter plates. This area is also prone to tsunamis.

An aerial view of the North Himalayan foothills shows a tectonic plate collision between the Indian Plate and the Asian Plate.

India experiences many earthquakes because of the Indian Tectonic Plate. This plate moves about 1.7 inches (4.3 centimeters) each year. Because the plate moves so much, it causes many earthquakes at its boundaries with nearby plates. The Indian Tectonic Plate is also responsible for earthquakes in Nepal. The plate has collided with another plate under Nepal and created a Himalayan fault where earthquakes frequently occur. Mexico also has frequent earthquakes. It sits on top of the Cocos Plate, the Pacific Plate, and the North American Plate.

FACT

The area where one tectonic plate moves under another tectonic plate and sinks into the Earth's mantle is called a **subduction** zone. These zones mark the collision between two tectonic plates.

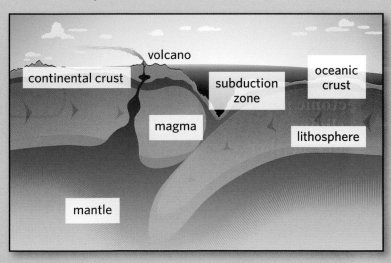

volcano

continental crust

subduction zone

oceanic crust

magma

lithosphere

mantle

subduction—the sinking of one plate edge beneath another

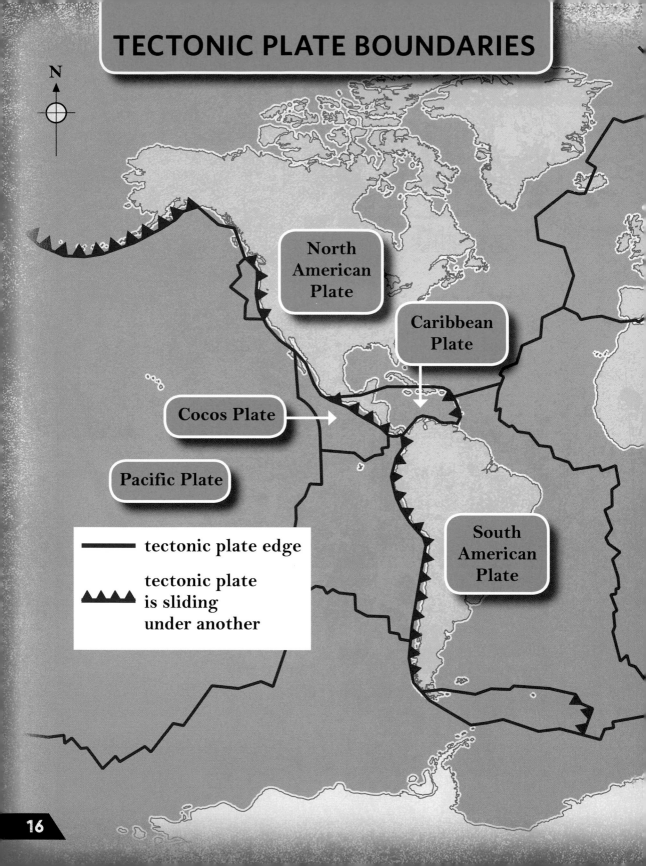

TECTONIC PLATE BOUNDARIES

N

North American Plate

Caribbean Plate

Cocos Plate

Pacific Plate

South American Plate

tectonic plate edge

tectonic plate is sliding under another

Eurasian Plate

Fiji Plate

African Plate

Indie-Australian Plate

Earth's continents are constantly moving
due to the motions of tectonic plates.

THE BIG ONES

One of the most damaging earthquakes in history took place in San Francisco, California, in 1906. It measured at 7.8 on the **Richter scale**. Many of the buildings at the time were made of wood and brick. Some were built on unstable ground. When the quake struck, buildings toppled. Fires broke out, destroying even more buildings. It is believed that more than 3,000 people died, although the exact number was never determined. More than 225,000 people were left homeless.

Another severe earthquake hit the San Francisco and Monterey Bay regions of California in 1989. It was a 7.1 **magnitude** quake and lasted 15 seconds. The quake was triggered by a slip in the San Andreas Fault system. The earthquake caused a freeway collapse and damaged the Oakland Bay Bridge.

FACT

The 1989 California earthquake happened during the third game of the baseball World Series in San Francisco. Much of the quake was captured on television as it happened.

Richter scale—a scale that helps scientists measure the energy released during an earthquake

magnitude—a measure of the amount of energy released by an earthquake

The two-level Cypress Freeway Structure collapsed during the 1989 earthquake near Oakland, California.

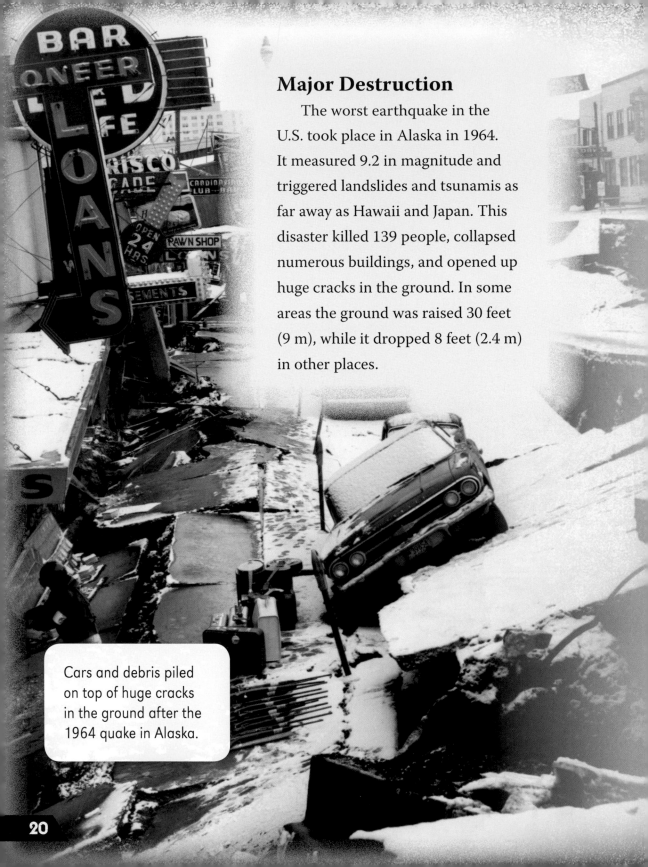

Major Destruction

The worst earthquake in the U.S. took place in Alaska in 1964. It measured 9.2 in magnitude and triggered landslides and tsunamis as far away as Hawaii and Japan. This disaster killed 139 people, collapsed numerous buildings, and opened up huge cracks in the ground. In some areas the ground was raised 30 feet (9 m), while it dropped 8 feet (2.4 m) in other places.

Cars and debris piled on top of huge cracks in the ground after the 1964 quake in Alaska.

A 1960 earthquake in Chile is the worst global quake on record. It measured 9.5 in magnitude. More than 1,600 people died as a result of the quake and the resulting tsunamis. The tsunami waves reached Hawaii and Japan, killing even more people and causing extensive damage. Two days later a volcano erupted in another part of Chile because of the quake.

The Puyehue volcano erupted in southern Chile in 2011 for the first time since the 1960 earthquake.

FACT

The New Madrid Fault Line is a major source of earthquakes in the southern and midwestern U.S.

Deaths, Damage, and Devastation

An earthquake took place off the island of Sumatra in Indonesia on December 26, 2004. It registered at a 9.1 on the Richter scale and released the same amount of energy as 23,000 atomic bombs. The undersea quake generated a giant tsunami wave more than 100 feet (30 m) high. The huge wave swept across the Pacific and affected 14 countries. The earthquake and tsunami was a deadly combination, causing 230,000 deaths.

A terrible earthquake hit Haiti on January 12, 2010. Because the ground under many buildings was made up of **sediment**, many poorly built buildings tumbled. About 200,000 people were killed. Many people were trapped under collapsed buildings, and there was no way to dig them out. One million people were left homeless. The airport was badly damaged too, which made it difficult to send rescuers to Haiti.

sediment—a mixture of tiny bits of rock, shells, plants, sand, and minerals

Before the Indonesian tsunami wave hit, many animals were seen moving to higher ground, including elephants. Few animal bodies were found in the wreckage.

People of Haiti walk through rubble where a building once stood after the 2010 quake.

MEASURING AND STUDYING EARTHQUAKES

Earthquakes are unpredictable. But scientists use tools to measure them. The Richter scale is a system developed in the 1930s. It measures the intensity of an earthquake. Earthquakes are classified on a scale of 1 to 10. Each number on the scale is 32 times stronger than the previous number. A quake measuring 2 on the Richter scale is barely felt. The largest, most damaging quake ever recorded had a magnitude of 9.5. It happened in southern Chile, South America.

The Richter scale is based on seismogram recordings. These recordings measure the vibrations from quakes.

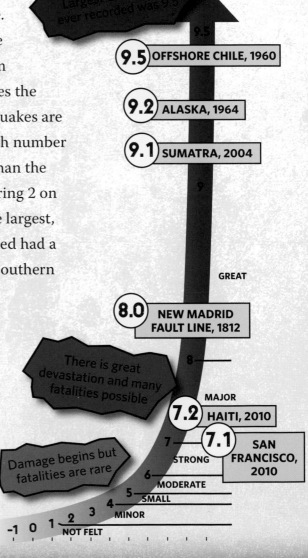

Largest earthquake ever recorded was 9.5

9.5 OFFSHORE CHILE, 1960

9.5

9.2 ALASKA, 1964

9.1 SUMATRA, 2004

9

GREAT

8.0 NEW MADRID FAULT LINE, 1812

There is great devastation and many fatalities possible

8

MAJOR

7.2 HAITI, 2010

7.1 SAN FRANCISCO, 2010

7

STRONG

Damage begins but fatalities are rare

6

MODERATE

5

SMALL

4

3

MINOR

2

1 0 -1

NOT FELT

Another measurement tool for earthquakes is a seismometer. A seismometer measures the strength, duration, and frequency of seismic waves during a quake. This instrument can also measure tremors that are too small to feel. Seismometers are set up underground where seismic activity is known to occur. Scientists monitor the recordings and data.

Seismometers are also used to measure seismic waves from nuclear explosions and asteroid impacts.

Developing Better Warnings

Scientists study earthquakes in hopes of finding ways to predict them. Even a little warning might help people get to a safe place. A team from NASA has developed new **radar** mapping technology. The radar map shows what faults look like during an earthquake. They can use this tool to take measurements and develop earthquake maps. These maps could show how fault lines behave and what areas are most likely to have earthquakes.

The Gravity Field and Steady-State Ocean Circulation Explorer observes Earth's sea levels and earthquakes from space.

Scientists can also use tools to measure tiny changes in pressure. For example a tiltmeter is an instrument used to measure very small changes from the vertical level, either on the ground or in structures. They can tell if land is rising or settling. **Satellites** are used to collect data from many sources, such as radar and electromagnetic emissions. This data could possibly give advanced warning that a quake is about to take place.

TOAD FORECASTERS

Researchers have found evidence that the common toad might be able to predict earthquakes. In 2009 scientists were studying hundreds of toads gathered at a pond in Italy for their spring mating. Suddenly all the toads began leaving the area. The researchers could not figure out why. Days later a strong earthquake struck the region. The researchers think that the toads may have sensed changes in the pond water or the air because of the coming earthquake. They returned several days after the quake.

radar—a device that uses radio waves to track the location of objects

satellite—a spacecraft that circles Earth; satellites gather and send information

STAYING SAFE

Earthquakes are almost always unexpected. So what can people do to stay safe when one happens? First of all, when the shaking begins, do not run outside. It is safer to stay inside, away from falling or flying debris. It is also better to take cover under a large table or in the corner of an interior wall. Stay away from windows or anything else made of glass. Avoid standing near large light fixtures such as chandeliers, which might fall. A quake can occur in just seconds, so it is best to identify safe places in a home or building in advance.

It is important to get as low as possible and cover the head and neck. If a person is in bed when a quake begins, the best thing to do is stay in the bed, covering the head with a pillow for protection. The best place to be outside during an earthquake is an open area away from buildings, trees, bridges, or anything else that might fall down. It is also important to stop a car or other vehicle when the shaking begins. It should also be parked in an area away from anything that might fall.

Be Prepared for the Worst

Because earthquakes are unpredictable, the best way to deal with them is to prepare in advance. Heavy shelves and other items hanging on walls should be attached with strong bolts. Cabinet doors should latch to keep things from flying out. It is also helpful to have an earthquake emergency kit.

AN EMERGENCY KIT SHOULD HAVE:

- a flashlight and extra batteries

- a battery-powered or crank powered radio

- a cell phone

- water

- canned or dried food

- a dust mask to keep from breathing in dust

- a first aid kit

- access to tools such as a shovel, axe, hammer, and crowbar

GLOSSARY

aftershock (AF-tur-shok)—a small earthquake that follows a larger one

axis (AK-siss)—a straight line around which an object rotates

basin (BAY-suhn)—the low, flat part of an ocean's floor

convection (kuhn-VEK-shuhn)—the movement of heat through liquids and gases

epicenter (EP-uh-sent-ur)—the point on Earth's surface directly above the place where an earthquake occurs

fault (FAWLT)—a crack in the earth where two plates meet; earthquakes often occur along faults

fracking (FRACK-ing)—the process of injecting liquid at high pressure into rocks to force open existing cracks and extract oil or gas

magnitude (MAG-nuh-tood)—a measure of the amount of energy released by an earthquake

mantle (MAN-tuhl)—the layer of super-hot rock that surrounds Earth's core

radar (RAY-dar)—a device that uses radio waves to track the location of objects

Richter scale (RIK-tuhr SKALE)—a scale that helps scientists measure the energy released during an earthquake

satellite (SAT-uh-lite)—a spacecraft that circles Earth; satellites gather and send information

sediment (SED-uh-muhnt)—a mixture of tiny bits of rock, shells, plants, sand, and minerals

seismic wave (SIZE-mik WAYV)—a wave of energy created by an earthquake

subduction (suhb-DUK-shuhn)—the sinking of one plate edge beneath another

tectonic plate (tek-TON-ik PLAYTE)—one of many gigantic slabs of Earth's crust that move around on magma

READ MORE

Collins, Terry. *Buried in Rubble: True Stories of Surviving Earthquakes.* True Stories of Survival. North Mankato, Minn.: Capstone Press, 2016.

Katirgis, Jane and Michele Ingber Drohan. *Eerie Earthquakes.* Earth's Natural Disasters. New York: Enslow Publishing, 2016.

Sepahban, Lois. *The Science of an Earthquake.* Disaster Science. Ann Arbor, Mich.: Cherry Lake Publishing, 2015.

INTERNET SITES

FactHound offers a safe, fun way to find Internet sites related to this book. All of the sites on FactHound have been researched by our staff.

Here's all you do:

Visit *www.facthound.com*

Type in this code: 9781515740384

Check out projects, games and lots more at
www.capstonekids.com

CRITICAL THINKING USING THE COMMON CORE

1. What is something that humans are doing that increases the chances for earthquakes occurring? (Key Ideas and Details)

2. What do tectonic plates have to do with earthquakes? (Integration of Knowledge and Ideas)

3. What is the Ring of Fire, and why do earthquakes happen there? (Key Ideas and Details)

INDEX